# A Coat of Flying Colours

## Passing Your Exams

### Bedtime Healing Meditation for Children

Little Blue Zen

# A Coat of Flying Colours

## Copyright@ 2024 Jo Galloway

The right of the author has been asserted to her following the copyright writing, designs and patent act of Australia.

All rights reserved. No part of this book may be reproduced, stored or transmitted by any means whether auditory, graphic, mechanical, or electronic without the written permission of the author. Unauthorised reproduction of any part of this work is illegal and is punishable by law.

Unless otherwise noted, the author and the publisher make no explicit guarantees as the accuracy of the information contained in this book may differ based on individual experiences and context

ISBN: 978-1-7635801-4-5

Published by Little Blue Zen
Birdwood NSW
Printed in Australia
Cover Design: Gagan Karunachandr
Editing: Kristine Gibson
jo@littlebluezen.com
http://www.littlebluezen.com

# A Coat of Flying Colours

## Bedtime Healing Meditation for Children

# Jo Galloway

### Your child may like other books in this series

- Bully Proof. Keeping out the bullies.

- I am Different, I am Me.

- The Magical Treasure Hunt. Building Confidence.

- The Magical Worry Balloon.

- Angelic Dreams. Meet your Guardian Angel.

- Scared of the Dark.

- I Love School.

- Bedwetting. Dry Nights.

Little Blue Zen.com

# INTRODUCTION

## Why Healing Meditations.

As children we make sense of our experiences based on our limited understanding and perception. We may misinterpret events or draw conclusions that form the basis of limiting beliefs that influence our entire life. These beliefs become ingrained over time, shaping our thoughts, feelings and behaviours well into adulthood unless consciously challenged.

In my work as a practising Hypnotherapist, I've found that all my clients' concerns, whether rooted in fears, feelings of inadequacy, addictive behaviours, or other challenges, trace back to their early childhood experiences, interactions, and upbringing. It's important to note that these issues don't exclusively stem from abusive or dysfunctional environments; limiting beliefs can arise from various circumstances.

Parents or caregivers wield substantial influence in shaping our perceptions of ourselves and the world around us. Remarks, criticisms, or comparisons made by family members can foster beliefs about our capabilities, worthiness, or potential. Furthermore, interactions with peers, teachers, and authority figures also contribute to the formation of these beliefs. Repeated experiences of rejection or failure can solidify beliefs such as "I'm not good enough" or "I'm unworthy of love."

This realzsation ignited my passion for intervening at the source: working with children to prevent these beliefs from taking root and manifesting into significant challenges in adulthood. By addressing issues early on, we can guide children to develop into the best versions of themselves, free from the burden of limiting beliefs that could otherwise dominate their lives.

.

## How Healing Meditation will help your child.

Teaching children meditation offers a multitude of benefits that can positively influence their daily lives and overall development. A regular mindfulness meditation practice provides valuable tools for managing stress, navigating emotions, and promoting overall well-being. Healing meditations, in particular, bolster your child's self-belief, helping to remove any resistance they may face in adulthood. This leads to a happier, more successful and fulfilling life.

Unlike traditional meditation, which often centres on relaxation, healing meditations go a step further by focusing on recovery, balance, and reprogramming a child's self-belief. These meditations use techniques such as breathing exercises, visualization, and guided imagery to not only foster deep relaxation but also reshape their mindset.

This targeted approach helps build a stronger sense of self-confidence and resilience. By integrating positive affirmations and emotional healing, healing meditations offer a distinct advantage over traditional methods, laying a powerful foundation for a child's future success and well-being.

Meditation can also be an effective part of your child's bedtime routine, helping to calm the mind and prepare the body for restful sleep. Techniques like guided imagery and deep breathing, as outlined in this book, can signal to the brain that it's time to wind down.

Sharing these calming moments at bedtime not only strengthens the bond between parent and child, but also creates a supportive and nurturing environment. It also sets a positive example, emphasizing the importance of self-care and mindfulness.

With patience and consistency, you can help your child develop a lifelong practice that supports their mental, emotional, and physical health. Give your child the gift of relaxation and imagination with this easy-to-read story designed to inspire and uplift.

# A Coat of Flying Colours

Sitting exams can often bring to the surface a child's self-sabotaging beliefs of "I'm not good enough," fears of failure or fear of rejection, along with bucket loads of anxiety.

Wearing the magical coat of Flying Colours is like wearing Superman's cape. This coat will transform your child's inner beliefs, allow access to their phenomenal memory and enable them to remain calm and in control while undertaking any exam.

No exam will ever cause worry or anxiety again. This magical healing, meditation will empower your child to do their absolute best, easily, naturally and brilliantly.

This magical coat holds within every thread everything they need to achieve and succeed. Allow this gentle meditation to ease their worries, enhance their belief in their capabilities, empower their positivity to pass every exam with flying colours.

This soothing meditation gently lulls your child to sleep while planting positive suggestions in their subconscious mind. Children have incredible imaginations and absorb these suggestions easily, which can lead to significant positive changes in their lives.

This story address inner worries that may be behind difficult or unusual behaviour's, fostering a sense of security, happiness and confidence.

Our mind learns by repetition so the more often your child listens to this magical story the better the effects. Delivered in a slow, monotone voice, this story captivates and soothes. A COAT OF FLYING COLOURS, is also available on YouTube, providing a soothing auditory experience children can enjoy at home, in the car, or anywhere they need a moment of relaxation.

**Listen on YouTube**

# A Coat of Flying Colours

Are you ready for a wonderful adventure my beautiful Little Starlight?

Snuggle up and settle down.

Make yourself really comfortable, have a little wriggle, and find the perfect spot.

When you're ready, uncross your legs and place your hands gently by your side.

Now, lay nice and still, softly close your eyes while your body begins to gently relax.

Your body is now sinking down into your warm, cozy bed.

You're feeling all floppy and floaty, snug, warm and safe.

Now, in your brilliant mind, imagine a bright, magical, rainbow light hovering above your head.

This magical light is spinning round and round, ever so slowly.

As it spins, it changes colour, from red to orange, to yellow, then green.

It is now turning a beautiful soft blue and then fading into violet.

It is now a shimmering crystal white light.

Every time you breathe in, you draw this magical white light down into your body.

Feel the magical light entering through the top of your head, gently flowing over your face.

It spreads down over your shoulders and continues down both arms, reaching all the way to the very tips of your fingers.

As it moves, you can feel a wonderful tingling sensation in your fingers.

The magical white light fills up your chest, slowly moving down your body and filling your tummy.

Your tummy feels all warm and calm.

You continue to breathe deep and slow, in and out.

This sparkly, shimmering white light now travels down your legs.

First down your right leg, then down your left leg, flowing through your feet and reaching all the way into your toes.

You might notice a delightful tingling sensation in your toes.

Your whole body is now bathed in this beautiful, crystal white light, filling you with a sense of radiant energy inside and outside.

Now, take a slow breath in through your nose.

As you exhale, gently breathe out, releasing the magical light from your body.

Watch as the sparkling light cascades around you.

You are now surrounded in a bubble of magical, shimmering, crystal white light.

This magical bubble lifts you gently, and you float up into the clouds.

As you sail through the sky, you feel completely safe inside your bubble of magical, crystal white light.

You soar high above the houses, rivers, and parks, bouncing from cloud to cloud.

You're having a wonderful time, smiling brightly as you listen to the birds singing as they flutter past.

You look down as you pass over your school and remember today is an incredibly special day, a day of exams.

Today you sit for a very important test.

You know it is time now, time to return home and get ready for school.

As I count down from ten to one, you will feel your magical crystal bubble slowly descend, bouncing from cloud to cloud as you make your way down.

Ten, feel yourself moving down, drifting down, sinking down.

Nine, landing softly on each fluffy cloud, as you slowly descend.

Eight, going deeper and deeper as you drift further down.

Seven and six, floating gently over the rooftops.

Five, gliding down, feeling calm, safe and relaxed.

Four, becoming sleepier and sleepier.

Three, almost at the bottom, feeling very peaceful.

Two, your bubble is landing softly.

One, you are safely back in your room.

It's now morning and time to get dressed and ready for school.

It is freezing outside, so you put on your uniform and your old worn-out coat.

Your coat feels heavy, dragging your shoulders down, and is extremely uncomfortable to wear.

It's scratchy and itchy and seems to hold in all your fears, doubts, and worries.

This coat carries your anxieties about whether you've studied enough for your exams today.

Doubts of whether you will pass and fears of failure.

Fears of not being good enough and thoughts of not being smart enough.

You're thinking, "I'm going to fail.
I've forgotten everything I have learned.
My brain is tired; I should have studied harder."
The pockets of your coat are overflowing with worry, anxiety and anger.
Unhappy feelings that make your stomach feel all yukky.
You feel sick, with a million butterflies dancing inside your tummy.
You really wish you could stay in bed and skip school today.
You hate exams.

This coat is a burden, but you wear it to school every day.

But today you decide to wear a different coat.

See yourself unbuttoning or unzipping your old ugly, heavy coat.

Shrug it off your shoulders and watch it drop to the floor.

You bend down to pick it up and then put it back in the cupboard.

You do not want that miserable, horrible coat of worries anymore.

You notice lying on the end of your bed a new coat.

This new coat is in your favourite colours.

You reach over and pick it up; It feels incredibly warm and soft, softer than a bunny rabbit's tail.

This is the most magnificent coat you have ever seen.

You drape it over your shoulders, pull the hood up over your head, and adjust the sleeves around your wrists.

As you wrap yourself in this brilliant coat, you feel special, clever and talented.

You're incredibly smart and look amazing, too.

Your new magical coat was made just for you, fitting perfectly like Cinderella's slipper.

Feeling snug as a bug in a rug.

You tie the belt around your waist, embracing your new coat of flying colours.

It feels so soft and snuggly and it even has your initials stitched into the front pocket.

In your new coat, you feel like a champion.

You feel all calm, confident and relaxed.

You can concentrate brilliantly now, and you will remember everything with ease.

All your worries about your exams vanish as if by magic.

You have an amazing memory that helps you shine.

Today, all the right answers come to you effortlessly.

You feel focused and ready to do your absolute best.

Wearing your magnificent coat of flying colours, you believe in yourself with all your heart.

You know you're going to do your best.

All your nerves and worries have disappeared, vanished, tucked away in your old coat.

Now, you're bubbling with excited about your exams.

When you look in the mirror, you notice something different about you.

But what could it be?

Is it the way you're standing?

Or maybe it's the way you look so confident, more focused, and happier?

I wonder who will be the first to notice the new you.

Will it be your teachers, your friends, or perhaps your parents?

Take a moment to notice how wonderful you feel in your new coat.

You now feel calm and confident, ready to excel in every test.

You're relaxed, focused, and completely in control.

All your worries have vanished.

Your new coat has many pockets, each filled with special talents and lessons.

One pocket is filled with confidence.

You know you are good enough, smart enough, and very clever.

Another pocket holds your amazing memory.

You will remember everything you need for your tests, everything you've studied for.

Your memory is incredibly sharp!

You are ready to shine.

There is also a pocket full of knowledge, packed with everything you have ever learned.

You're a walking, talking genius - smart, clever and talented.

One pocket holds faith, assuring you will pass all your exams easily and effortlessly, with flying colours, not a doubt in sight.

Peace fills another pocket, helping you to stay cool, calm and collected.

No more butterflies in your stomach- just calm confidence.

You are relaxed and ready for anything.

Finally, you have a pocket full of Angels, guiding and protecting you.

They are here to help you whenever you need them, offering support and holding your hand.

Your Angels love to offer you assistance!

All you have to do is ask.

You feel happy now, knowing that you have everything you need to shine like a star.

You are so very proud of yourself.

You are amazing.

Wearing your coat of flying colours, you shine.

You can see yourself sitting at your desk, waiting for the exam to start.

You feel happy and confident knowing you're wearing your super magical coat of flying colours.

As your exam begins, the answers come to you effortlessly from inside your mind.

Wow, "that was easy!" you say with a smile as you hand in your finished exam.

Now you know before every exam or test, all you need to do is close your eyes, put on your magical coat of flying colours, and all your nerves and worries will be gone.

You know you will do your absolute best.

Now that you're ready, there are no more upset tummies, no more fears of failing, no more tossing and turning in bed at night.

You can rest peacefully, knowing that you will breeze through your next exams with ease.

Good luck, little Starlight—go out and shine!

In the morning, you'll wake up feeling confident, happy, calm and back in control.

You've got this, you can do this.

You are unstoppable.

So, knowing this and believing this, you can now peacefully and effortlessly drift off to sleep.

As you rest, you'll dream the most magical dreams, seeing A+ on every exam paper.

You are a champion.

Well done, little Starlight.

Sweet dreams…………..

# Also by Jo Galloway

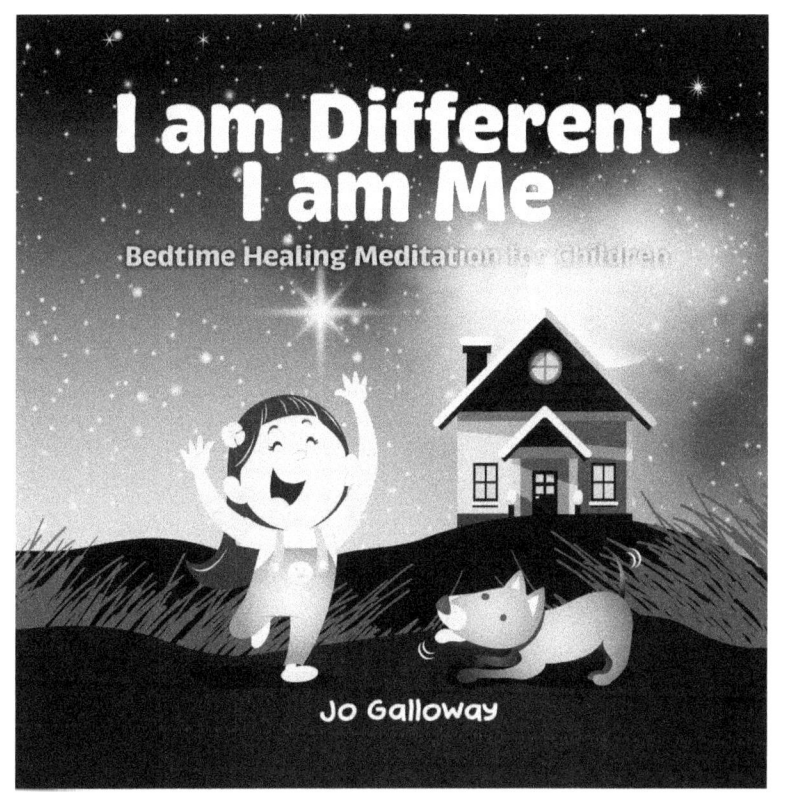

In a world where everyone is unique and special, being different is something to celebrate! "I Am Different, I Am Me" is a delightful bedtime story that shows just how wonderful it is to be yourself.

It's all about embracing our differences, celebrating our uniqueness, and feeling proud of who we are. This empowering meditation encourages your child to embrace their individuality and recognize their special gifts. They will discover the joy of being exactly who they were meant to be.

Give your child the gift of imagination and relaxation at bedtime with this easy-to-read story, designed to inspire and uplift.

www.ingramcontent.com/pod-product-compliance
Lightning Source LLC
Chambersburg PA
CBHW042355070526
44585CB00028B/2945